# Perugia
# Italy

## City Map

⊕ Glob:us

**Perugia, Italy — City Map**
By Jason Patrick Bates

First Edition: October 2017

**Scale** / 1:4000

| 50m

| 500ft

Map Overview

## Map Symbols

| | | | | |
|---|---|---|---|---|
| ▬ | Highway | ⬢ | Map continuation page | |
| ▬ | Street | ···· | Path | |

| | | | | |
|---|---|---|---|---|
| 🏆 | Archaeological site | ▦ | Kiosk | |
| ♟ | Artwork | ✕ | Level crossing | |
| 🏧 | Atm | 📖 | Library | |
| ▼ | Bar | 🗼 | Lighthouse | |
| 🚲 | Bicycle rental | ▤ | Memorial | |
| 🍺 | Biergarten | ▦ | Memorial plaque | |
| ☸ | Buddhist temple | ⚉ | Monument | |
| 🚌 | Bus station | 🏛 | Museum | |
| 🚏 | Bus stop | ☪ | Muslim mosque | |
| ☕ | Cafe | ▦ | Neighbourhood | |
| ⛺ | Camping site | ♫ | Nightclub | |
| 🚗 | Car rental | Ⓟ | Parking | |
| ◠ | Cave entrance | ▲ | Peak | |
| 🏠 | Chalet | ⚕ | Pharmacy | |
| ⚡ | Charging station | ⚶ | Picnic site | |
| † | Church / Monastery | 🛝 | Playground | |
| 🎬 | Cinema | 👮 | Police | |
| ⚖ | Courthouse | ✉ | Post office | |
| 🏬 | Department store | ▥ | Prison | |
| 🐾 | Dog park | 🍺 | Pub | |
| 🚰 | Drinking water | 🚉 | Railway | |
| 🧺 | Dry cleaning | 🍴 | Restaurant | |
| 🛗 | Elevator | ⛩ | Shinto temple | |
| 🏴 | Embassy | ☯ | Sikh temple | |
| 🍔 | Fast food | 🏃 | Sports centre | |
| ⚓ | Ferry terminal | 🛒 | Supermarket | |
| 🔥 | Fire station | ☯ | Taoist temple | |
| ⛲ | Fountain | 🚕 | Taxi | |
| ⛽ | Fuel | ☎ | Telephone | |
| 🏌 | Golf course | 🎭 | Theatre | |
| 🏨 | Guest house | 🚻 | Toilets | |
| ॐ | Hindu temple | 🏛 | Townhall | |
| ⊕ | Hospital | 🚦 | Traffic signals | |
| 🏨 | Hostel | ❋ | Viewpoint | |
| 🏨 | Hotel | 🏄 | Water park | |
| i | Information | 🏕 | Wilderness hut | |
| ✡ | Jewish synagogue | ✕ | Windmill | |

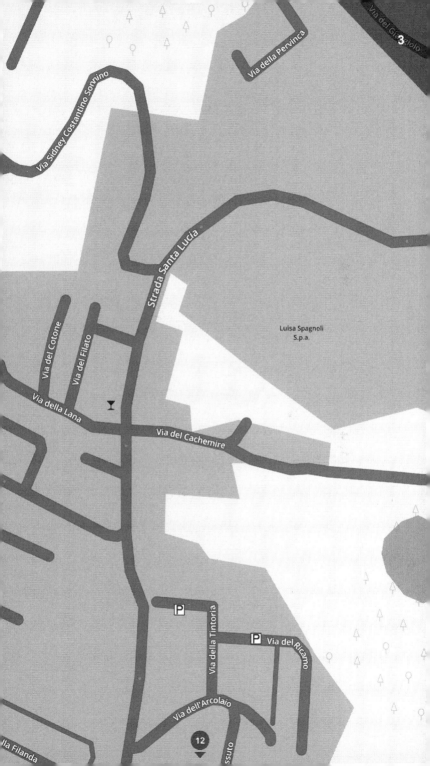

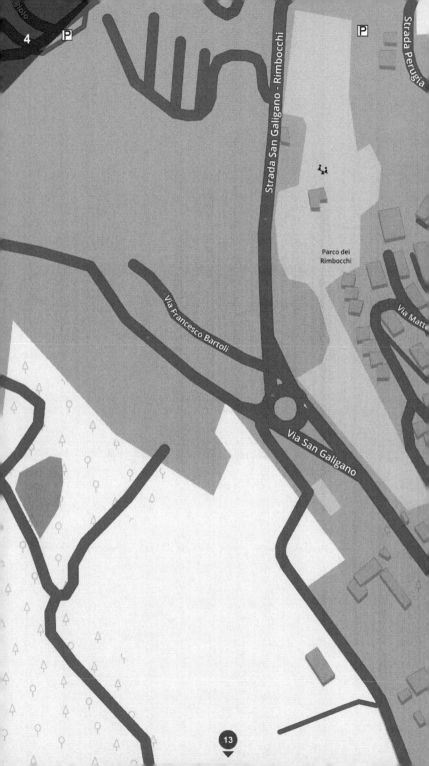

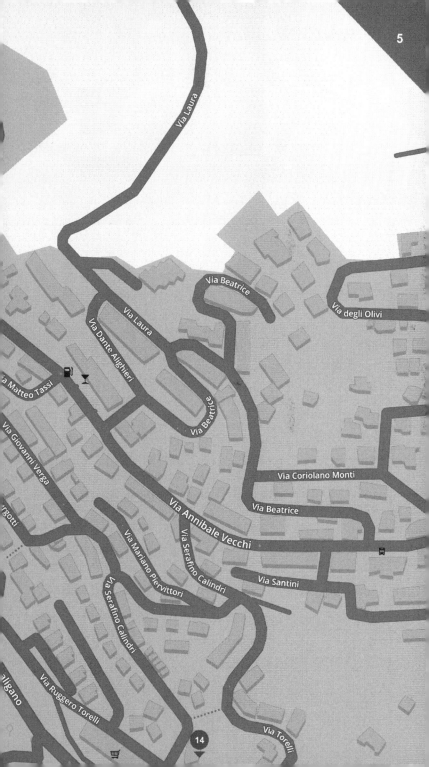

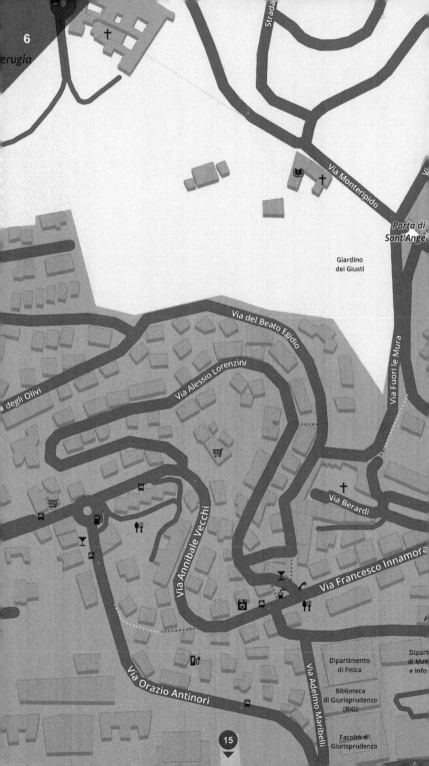

Via Sperandio

Via Sperandio

i Tempio

baldi

Via Fra' Andrea da Perugia

Via Benedetta

Via Zefferino Faina

Corso Giuseppe Garibaldi

Via Lucida

Via dell'Oro

Parco Sant'Angelo

P

a Francesco Innamorati

Aula Magna

Stazione
CC Perugia
Fortebraccio
Rettorato

P

Via del Fagiano

Via del Gallo

Via dei Pellari

i Sotto

Facoltà di
Economia
e Scienze
Politiche

Farmacia

Via del Liceo

Via Pulignani

Via Ariodante Fabretti

Via del Bulagaio

Via della Per

16

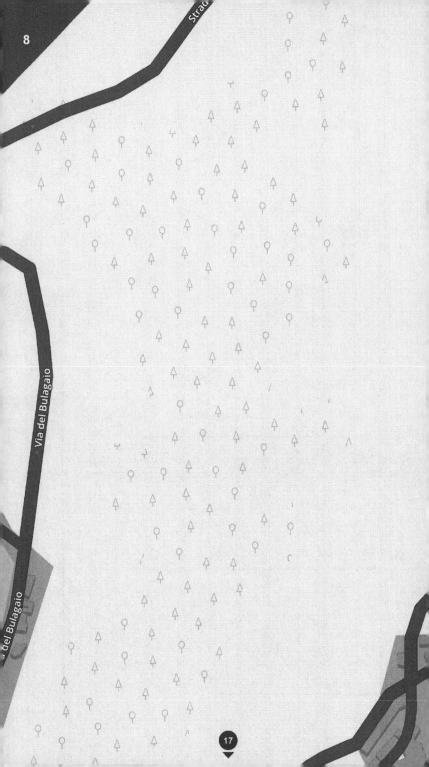

Strada

Via del Bulagaio

del Bulagaio

Viale

Pista Bmx

Percorso
Verde

Laghetto
del Percorso
verde

Viale Pietro Conti

P

P

elli Cairoli

P

18

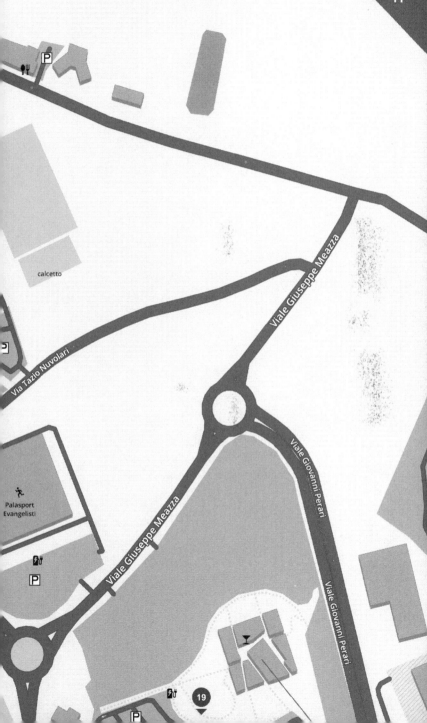

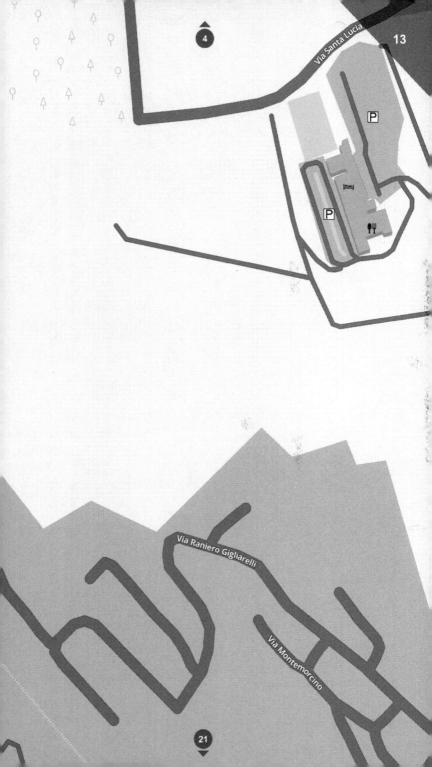

Via Raniero Gigliarelli

Via Montemorcino

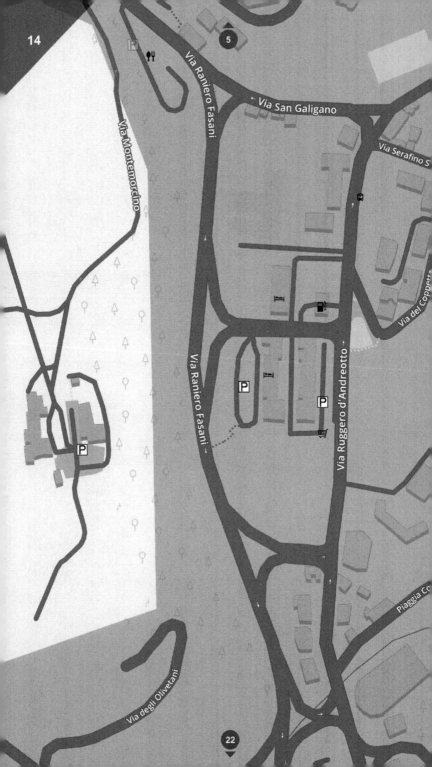

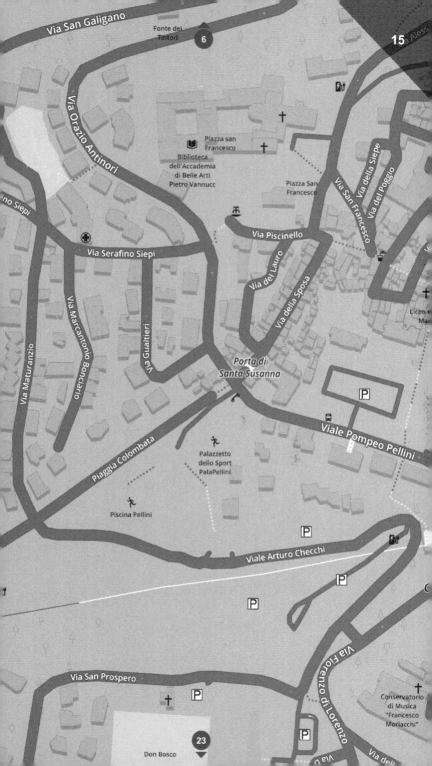

Fonte dei Tintori

6

Via Orazio Antinori

Piazza san Francesco

Biblioteca dell'Accademia di Belle Arti Pietro Vannucc

Piazza San Francesco

Via della Siepe

Via San Francesco

Via del Poggio

Via Serafino Siepi

Via Piscinello

Liceo Ma

no Siepi

Via del Lauro

Via della Sposa

Via Maturanzio

Via Marcantonio Bonciario

Via Gualtieri

Porta di Santa Susanna

P

Piaggia Colombata

Palazzetto dello Sport PalaPellini

Viale Pompeo Pellini

P

Piscina Pellini

P

Viale Arturo Checchi

P

P

Via Fiorenzo di Lorenzo

Via San Prospero

P

Conservatorio di Musica "Francesco Morlacchi"

P

23

Don Bosco

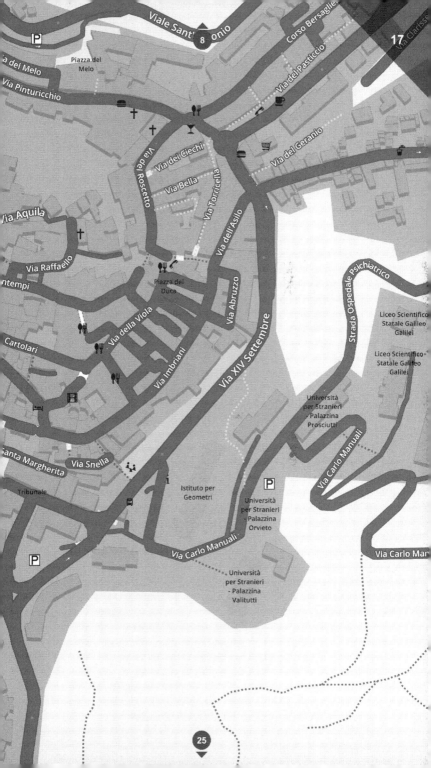

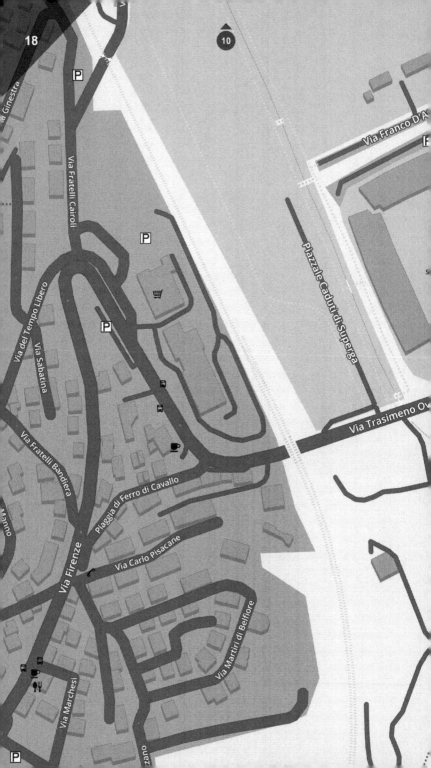

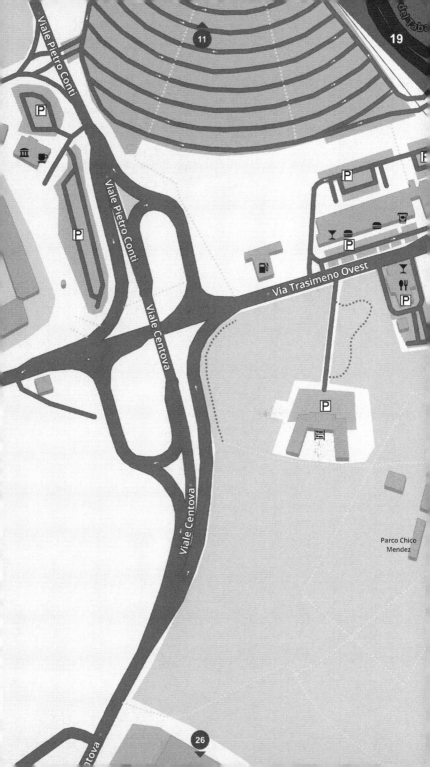

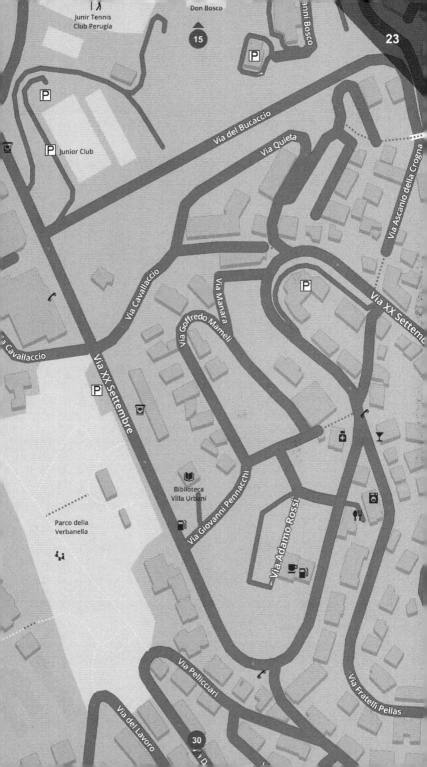

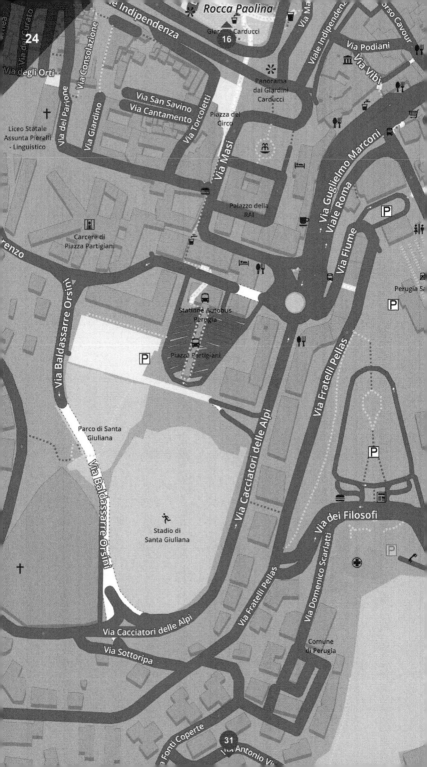

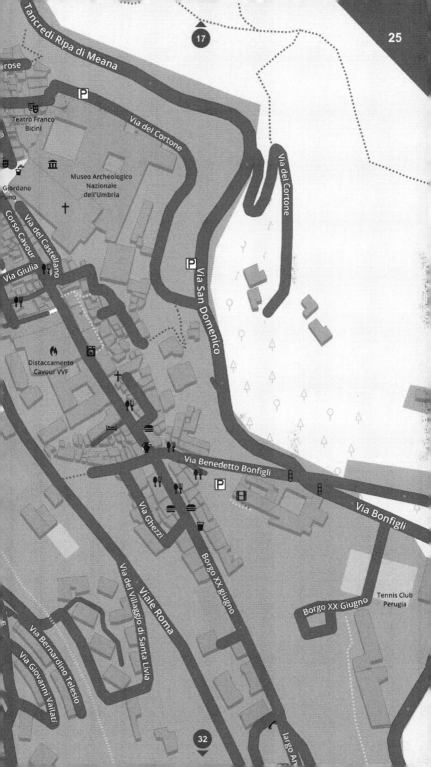

17

Tancredi Ripa di Meana

rose

Teatro Franco
Bicini

Via del Cortone

Museo Archeologico
Nazionale
dell'Umbria

Giordano
uno

Via del Cortone

Via del Cortone

Corso Cavour

Via del Castellano

Via Giulia

Via San Domenico

Distaccamento
Cavour VVF

Via Benedetto Bonfigli

Via Bonfigli

Via Ghezzi

Borgo XX giugno

Via del Villaggio di Santa Livia

Viale Roma

Borgo XX Giugno

Tennis Club
Perugia

Via Bernardino Telesio

Via Giovanni Vailati

largo An

32

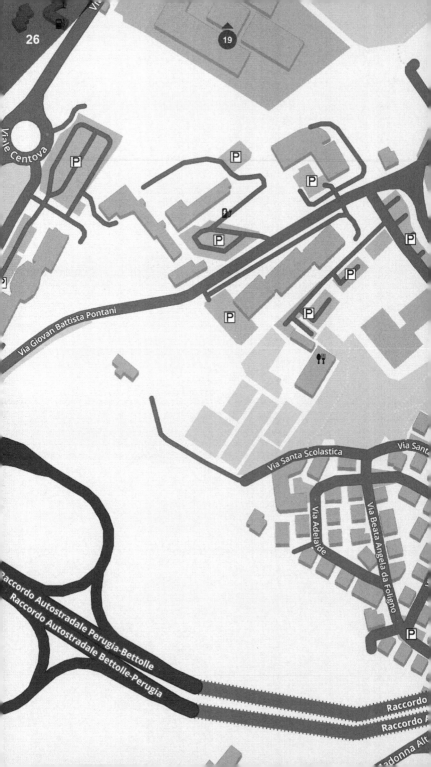

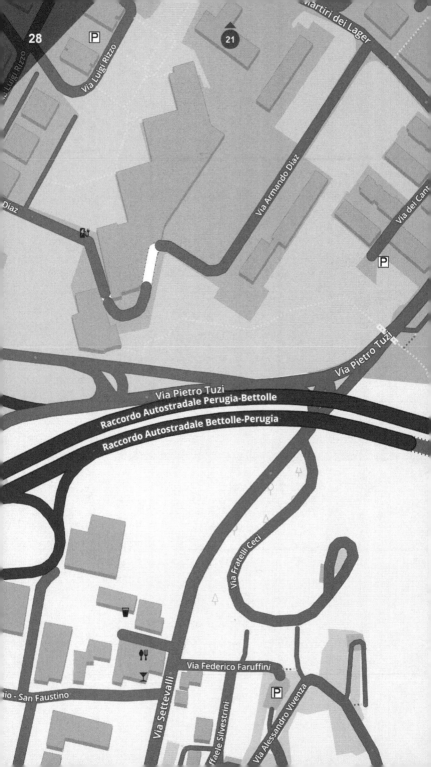

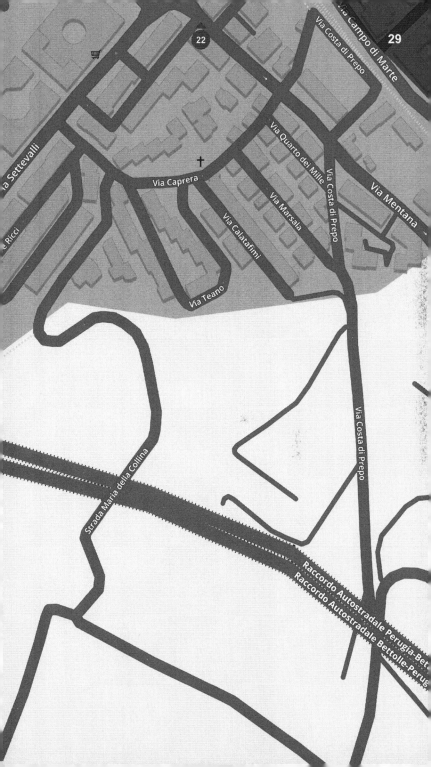

23

Fontivegge

Via del Lavoro

Via Filippo Lardoni

Girolamo Bigazzini

Rosselli

Via de

Via del Lavoro

Via Campo di Marte

Via Campo di Marte

Via Campo di

Via Mentana

Via del Palio

Via della Balestra

Via della Quintana

25

Via Cesare Balbo

Via Bratislava

Borgo XX giugno

✝

Giardini del
Frontone

Orto Botan

Porta San
Costanzo

Via dei Filosofi

Via San Bonaventura

Via Roma

Copacabana
mercatino
dell'usato

Orto Botanico

Centro Servizi Pietro Grocco

Galileo Galilei

otta

Pellico

Via d

Via Romana

Perugia-Bettolle

olle-Perugia

Via Mater Dei

Sport Complex
- Stadium
- UniPG

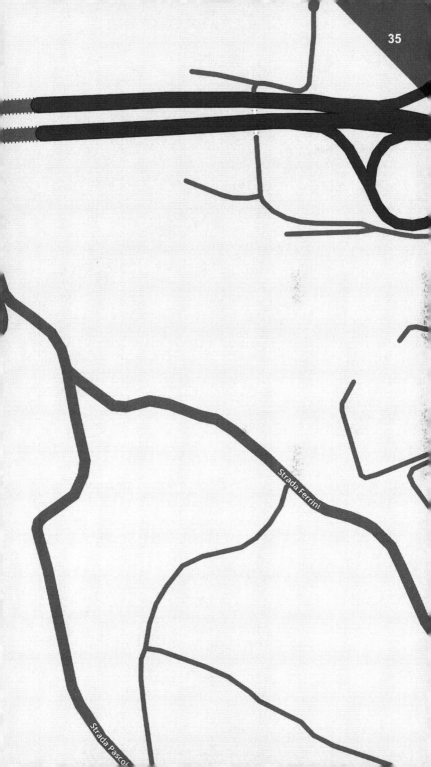

Strada Ferrini

Strada Pascol

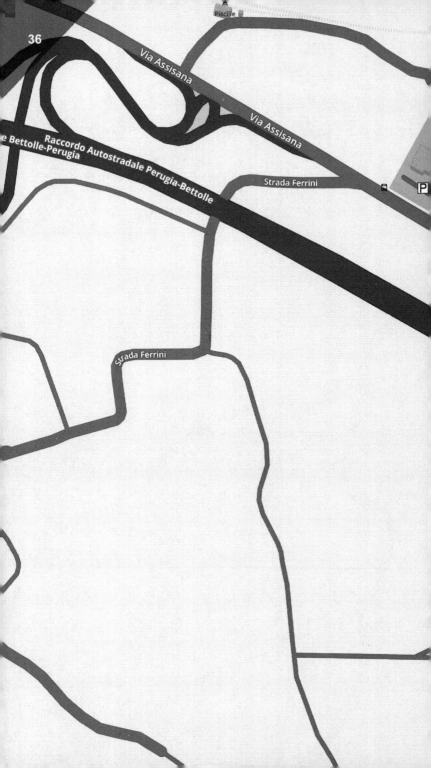

ITTS Alessandro
Volta

P

P

Raccordo Autostradale
Raccordo Autostrada

Via Assisana

gia-Bettolle

ettolle-Perugia

Raccordo Autostradale Bettolle-Perugia

P

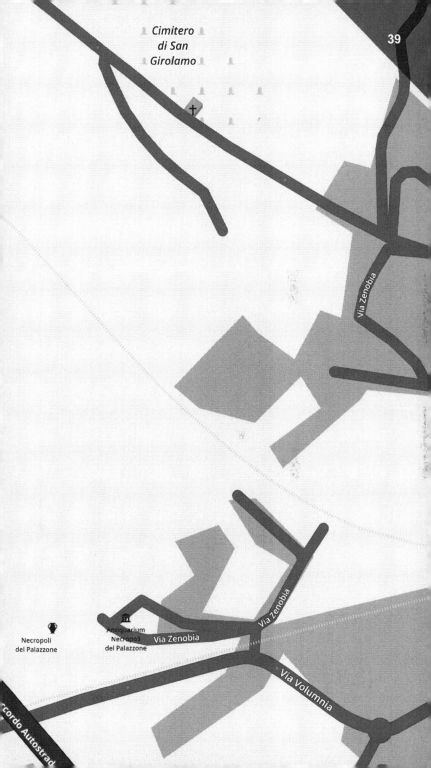

Cimitero
di San
Girolamo

Via Zenobia

Via Zenobia

Antiquarium
Necropoli
del Palazzone

Via Zenobia

Necropoli
del Palazzone

Via Volumnia

cordo Autostrad

40

# Streets

## B

Borgo xx giugno . . 25, 32

## C

Centro servizi pietro
    grocco . . . . . . 32, 33
Corso bersaglieri . . 8, 17
Corso cavour . . 16, 24, 25
Corso giuseppe
    garibaldi . . . . . . . 6, 7
Corso vannucci . . . . . . 16

## E

Entrata segreterie . . . . 33

## G

Galleria john fitzgerald
    kennedy . . . . . . . . 16
Giardini di piazza italia16

## L

Largo antonio brizi25, 32
Largo cacciatori delle
    alpi . . . . . . . . . . . . . 24
Largo della libertà 16, 24
Largo leone xiii . . . . . . 22
Largo madonna alta . 27

## P

P.zza dell'università . . . 7
Piaggia colombata 14, 15
Piaggia dei filosofi 24, 25
Piaggia della torre . . . . 6
Piaggia di ferro di cav-
    allo . . . . . . . . . . . . . 18

Piazza annibale mariotti
    15, 16
Piazza braccio forte-
    braccio . . . . . . . . . . . 7,
    16
Piazza cavallotti . . . . . . 16
Piazza danti . . . . . . . . . . 16
Piazza del bacio - pi-
    azza nuova . . . . . . 22
Piazza del circo . . . . . . 24
Piazza del drago . . . . . 16
Piazza del duca . . . . . . 17
Piazza del melo . . . . . . 17
Piazza del porcellino . . 8
Piazza dell'università . . 7
Piazza della repubblica
    16
Piazza di monteluce . . 9
Piazza domenico lu-
    patelli . . . . . . . . . . . . 7
Piazza domenico lupat-
    telli . . . . . . . . . . . . . . 7
Piazza fonti di veggio 22,
    23
Piazza gabriele
    d'annunzio . . . 31, 32
Piazza gian battista
    rossi scotti . . . 16, 17
Piazza giordano bruno
    25
Piazza giuseppe ermini
    16
Piazza grimana . . . . . . 16
Piazza italia . . . . . . . . . 16
Piazza iv novembre . . 16
Piazza matteotti . . . . . . 16
Piazza morlacchi . . . . . 16
Piazza piccinino . . . . . . 16
Piazza san giovanni di
    dio . . . . . . . . . . . . . 24
Piazza san paolo . . 15, 16
Piazza umbria jazz . . . . 11
Piazza vittorio veneto 22

Piazzale anna frank . . 31
Piazzale caduti di su-
    perga . . . . . . . . . . . 18
Piazzale giotto . . . . . . . 31

## R

Raccordo autostradale
    bettolle-perugia
    26–29, 35–38
Raccordo autostradale
    perugia-bettolle
    26–29, 35–38

## S

Scale adelmo maribelli
    6
Sport complex pedes-
    trian path . . . . . . . . 34
Strada bellocchio - san
    faustino . . . . . . 27, 28
Strada case bruciate
    santa lucia . . . . . . . 13
Strada dei lambrelli . . . 9
Strada dei loggi . . . . . . 39
Strada del borghetto . 30
Strada del brozzo . . . . 34
Strada del rio . . . . . . . . . 6
Strada della pallotta . 33
Strada di san vetturino
    34
Strada ferrini . . . . . 35, 36
Strada maria della col-
    lina . . . . . . . . . . . . . 29
Strada ospedale psichi-
    atrico . . . . . . . . . . . 17
Strada pascoletti . . . . . 35
Strada perugia - san
    marco . . . . . . . . . . 4, 5
Strada perugia ponte rio
    7, 8

42

Strada pian della genna
20, 21, 26, 27
Strada san galigano -
rimbocchi . . . . . . . . 4
Strada santa lucia . . 3, 4,
12
Strada santa lucia civ. 2
12
Strada trasimeno ovest
19
Strada vicinale del bel-
locchio . . . . . . . . . 22

---

**T**

Traversa via romana . 32,
33

---

**V**

Via a. fratti . . . . . . . . . . 16
Via abruzzo . . . . . . . . . 17
Via achille grandi . 26, 27
Via ada . . . . . . . . . . 26, 27
Via adamo rossi . . . . . . 23
Via adelaide . . . . . . . . 26
Via adelmo maribelli . . 6
Via adriana . . . . . . . . . . 21
Via agostino di duccio 9
Via alba . . . . . . . . . . . . . 16
Via alessandro arienti 28
Via alessandro pascoli6,
7, 15, 16
Via alessandro vivenza
28
Via alessio lorenzini . . . 6
Via alfredo cotani 20, 26,
27
Via alunni . . . . . . . . . . . 16
Via americo andreocci
15, 23
Via angusta . . . . . . . . . 17
Via annibale brugnoli . 8,
9, 17
Via annibale mariotti . 16
Via annibale spagnoli
detto lino . . . . . . . . 12
Via annibale vecchi . 5, 6
Via antonio mezzanotte
18
Via antonio pigafetta . 12
Via antonio salandra . . 3
Via antonio vivaldi 24, 31
Via appia . . . . . . . . . . . . 16
Via apponi . . . . . . . . . . 33
Via aquila . . . . . . . . . . 17
Via arcadia . . . . . . . . . . 30

Via ariodante fabretti . . 7
Via armando diaz . 27, 28
Via armonica . . . . . . 15, 16
Via arnolfo di cambio . 9
Via ascanio della
crogna . . . . . . . . . 23
Via assisana . . . . . . 33–38
Via azzi . . . . . . . . . . . . . 17
Via baglioni . . . . . . . . . 16
Via baldassarre orsini 24
Via baldeschi . . . . . . . . 16
Via baldo . . . . . . . . . . . . 16
Via bartolo . . . . . . . . . . 16
Via beata angela da
foligno . . . . . . . 26, 27
Via beatrice . . . . . . . . . . 5
Via bella . . . . . . . . . . . . 17
Via bellocchio . 21, 22, 29
Via benedetta . . . . . . . . 7
Via benedetto bonfigli
25
Via benincasa . . . . . . . 16
Via berardi . . . . . . . . . . . 6
Via berenice . . . . . . . . . 21
Via bernardino sozi . . 26,
27
Via bernardino telesio 25
Via bonaccia . . . . . . . . 17
Via boncambi . . . . . . . . 16
Via bonfigli . . . . 25, 32, 33
Via bontempi . . . . . 16, 17
Via borghetto di prepo
30, 31
Via bottinelli . . . . . . 16, 17
Via bovaro . . . . . . . . . . 16
Via bratislava . . . . . . . . 32
Via breve . . . . . . . . . . . . 22
Via brunamonti . . . . 9, 17
Via bruschi . . . . . . . . . . 16
Via cacciatori delle alpi
24
Via caduti del lavoro . 31
Via calatafimi . . . . . . . . 29
Via campo di battaglia
16
Via campo di marte . . 22,
23, 29–31
Via cantamento . . . . . . 24
Via caprera . . . . . . . . . . 29
Via carlo cattaneo . . . . . 9
Via carlo manuali . . . . 17
Via carlo pisacane . . . 18
Via cartolari . . . . . . 16, 17
Via case bruciate . 14, 21,
22
Via cavallaccio . . . . . . . 23
Via cesare balbo . . . . . 32

Via cesare battisti . . . . 16
Via cesare beccaria . 24,
25
Via cesare caporali . . . 16
Via cesare fani . . . . . . . 16
Via cesare massari . . . . 9
Via cesare pascarella 32
Via cesarei . . . . . . . . 16, 17
Via clarisse . . . . . . . . 9, 17
Via colomba . . . . . . . . . 25
Via colomba antonietti
29
Via consolazione . . . . . 24
Via coriolano monti . 5, 6
Via cortonese . 14, 20–22
Via costa di prepo . . . 29
Via cumana . . . . . . . . . . 16
Via curtatone e monta-
nara . . . . . . . . . . . . 22,
29
Via dall'arco . . . . . . . . . 15
Via dalmazio birago . 23,
30, 31
Via dante alighieri . . . . . 5
Via danzetta . . . . . . . . 16
Via degli apostoli . 15, 23,
24
Via degli archi . . . . . . . 25
Via degli offici . . . . . . . 16
Via degli olivetani . . . . 14
Via degli olivi . . . . . . . 5, 6
Via degli orti . . . . . . . . 24
Via degli sciri . . . . . . . . 15
Via degli scortici . . . 7, 16
Via dei barutoli . . . . . . . 7
Via dei cantoni . . . . . . 28
Via dei ciechi . . . . . . . . 17
Via dei filosofi . 24, 25, 32
Via dei gatti . . . . . . . . . 16
Via dei pellari . . . . . . . . 7
Via dei priori . . . . . 15, 16
Via del balcone . . . . . . 17
Via del beato egidio . . . 6
Via del bottone . . . . . . . 3
Via del bucaccio . . . . . 23
Via del bulagaio . . . . 7, 8
Via del cachemire . . . . . 3
Via del cane . . . . . . . . . 17
Via del canterino . . . . 25
Via del cardellino . . . . 16
Via del carmine . . . . . . 17
Via del castellano . . . . 25
Via del conventuccio 16,
17, 24, 25
Via del coppetta . . . . . 14
Via del cortone . . . 24, 25
Via del cotone . . . . . . . . 3

Via del curato . . . . . . . . 24
Via del dado . . . . . . . . 16
Via del deposito . . . . . 25
Via del duca . . . . . . . . . . 17
Via del fagiano . . . . . . . . 7
Via del filato . . . . . . . . . . 3
Via del fiordaliso . . . . . . 3
Via del forno . . . . . . . . . 16
Via del forte . . . . . . . . . . 16
Via del fumo . . . . . . . . . 17
Via del gallo . . . . . . . . . . 7
Via del geranio . . . . . . . 17
Via del giaggiolo . . . . 3, 4
Via del giochetto . . . . . . 9
Via del grillo . . . . . . . . . 25
Via del lauro . . . . . . . . . . 15
Via del lavoro . . . . . 23, 30
Via del liceo . . . . . . . . . . 7
Via del lupo . . . . . . . . . . 17
Via del macello . . 21, 22,
    29
Via del maneggio . . 7, 16
Via del melo . . . . . . . . . . 17
Via del moro . . . . . . . . . 7
Via del morone . . . . . . . 16
Via del palio . . . . . . . . . 30
Via del paradiso . . 16, 24
Via del parione . . . . . . . 24
Via del pasticcio . . . . . . 17
Via del pero . . . . . . . . . 16
Via del pioppo . . . . . . . . 6
Via del poeta . . . . . . 7, 16
Via del poggio . . . . . . . 15
Via del pozzo . . . . . . . . 16
Via del prospetto . . . . . 17
Via del ranuncolo . . . . . 3
Via del ricamo . . . . . . . . 3
Via del roscetto . . . . . . 17
Via del sacco . . . . . . . . . 17
Via del salto . . . . . . . . . . 17
Via del sette . . . . . . . . . 16
Via del silenzio . . . . . . . 16
Via del sole . . . . . . . 16, 17
Via del tabacchificio . 11,
    12, 19, 20
Via del tempio . . . . . . . . 7
Via del tempo libero . 18
Via del tessuto . . . . 3, 12
Via del topo . . . . . . . . . . 17
Via del toppo . . . . . . . . . 21
Via del verzaro . . . . . . . 16
Via del villaggio di
    santa livia . . . . . . . 25
Via deliziosa . . . . . . . . . 16
Via dell'acquedotto 7, 16
Via dell'angora 13, 21, 22
Via dell'aquilone . . . . . 16

Via dell'arcolaio . . . . . . . 3
Via dell'asilo . . . . . . . . . 17
Via dell'aurora . . . . . . . . 7
Via dell'oro . . . . . . . . . . . 7
Via della balestra . . . . 30
Via della brocca . . . . . . 16
Via della campana . . . 17
Via della cardatura . 3, 12
Via della cometa . . . . . . 7
Via della concordia . . 30,
    31
Via della cupa . . . . 15, 16
Via della ferrovia . . . . 22
Via della filanda . . . . 3, 12
Via della gabbia . . . . . . 16
Via della lana . . . . . . . . . 3
Via della luna . . . . . . . . 16
Via della madonna . . . 17
Via della moda . . . . . . . 3
Via della nespola . . . . 16
Via della pallotta . 31–33
Via della pergola . . 7, 16
Via della pernice . . . . 16
Via della pervinca . . . . . 3
Via della pescara 23, 30,
    31
Via della quintana . . . 30
Via della rupe . . . . . 16, 17
Via della scala . . . . . . . 17
Via della seta . . . . 10, 18
Via della siepe . . . . . . . 15
Via della sposa . . . . . . 15
Via della stella . . . . . . . 16
Via della tintoria . . . . . . 3
Via della viola . . . . . . . . 17
Via delle cantine . . . . 16
Via delle conce . . . . . . 17
Via delle forze . . . . 15, 24
Via delle prome . . . . . . 16
Via delle sorgenti . . . 4, 5
Via delle streghe . . . . . 16
Via dello struzzo . . . . . 16
Via dello stvrione . 16, 17
Via di loggia . . . . . . . . . . 7
Via di senso . . . . . . . . . . 7
Via domenico lupatelli 7
Via domenico lupattelli
    7
Via domenico scarlatti
    24
Via don giovanni bosco
    15, 23
Via donato bramante . . 9
Via eburnea . . . . . . 23, 24
Via elce di sotto . 6, 7, 16
Via eleonora . . . . . . 26, 27
Via enrico cialdini . . . 8, 9

Via enrico dal pozzo . . 17
Via enrico pestalozzi . . 9
Via enrico toti . . . . . . . 27
Via eremita . . . . . . . . . . 16
Via etrusca . . . . . . . . . . 39
Via ettore ricci . . . . . . 29
Via eugenio curiel . . . 26
Via eugenio oliveto . . 18
Via eugubina . . . . . . . . . 9
Via fatabenefratelli . . . 24
Via favorita . . . . . . . . . . 16
Via federico faruffini . . 28
Via filippo lardoni . . . . 30
Via fioramonti . . . . . . . 16
Via fiorenzo di lorenzo
    15, 16, 23, 24
Via fiorenzuola . . . 24, 25
Via firenze . . . . . . . . . . 18
Via fiume . . . . . . . . . . . . 24
Via fonti coperte . . 24, 31
Via fortunata . . . . . . . . . 7
Via fosso . . . . . . . . . . . . 21
Via fra' andrea da peru-
    gia . . . . . . . . . . . . . . 7,
    8
Via fra' bevignate . . . . . 9
Via francesco baracca
    27, 28
Via francesco bartoli . . 4
Via francesco briganti 21
Via francesco de sanc-
    tis . . . . . . . . . . . . . . . 9
Via francesco di giorgio
    9
Via francesco in-
    namorati . . . . . . . . 6,
    7
Via francesco moretti . 9
Via francesco petrarca
    31
Via franco d'attoma . . 18,
    19
Via francolina . . . . . 15, 16
Via fratelli bandiera . . 18
Via fratelli cairoli . 10, 18
Via fratelli ceci . . . . . . 28
Via fratelli pellas . 23, 24
Via fratelli purgotti . . 4, 5
Via fratelli rosselli 23, 30
Via fratti . . . . . . . . . . . . 16
Via frà giovanni da pian
    di carpine . . . . . . 18
Via fuori le mura . . . . . . 6
Via g. pierluigi da
    palestrina . . . . . . . 30
Via galeazzo alessi16, 17
Via galileo galilei . 31, 32

44

Via gentile . . . . . . . . . . . . 7
Via ghezzi . . . . . . . . . . . . 25
Via giancarlo connesta-
  bile . . . . . . . . . . . . . . 18
Via giardino . . . . . . . . . . 24
Via ginestra . . . . . . . . . . 18
Via giovan battista pon-
  tani . . . . . . . . . . . . . . 26
Via giovanni boccaccio
  31
Via giovanni cecchini 28
Via giovanni da veraz-
  zano . . . . . . . . . . . . . 18
Via giovanni pennacchi
  23
Via giovanni pierluigi da
  palestrina . . . . 30, 31
Via giovanni ruggia . . 30,
  31
Via giovanni vailati . . . 25
Via giovanni verga . . 4, 5
Via girolamo bigazzini
  23, 30
Via girolamo savonarola
  25, 31
Via girolamo tilli . . . . . . 20
Via gismonda . . . . . . . . 25
Via giulia . . . . . . . . . . . . 25
Via giuseppe bamba-
  gioni . . . . . . . . . . . . . 32
Via giuseppe busti . . . 22
Via giuseppe di vittorio
  27
Via giuseppe evange-
  listi . . . . . . . . . . . . . . 21
Via giuseppe lombardo
  radice . . . . . . . . . . . 31
Via giuseppe mazzini 16
Via goffredo duranti . . . 3
Via goffredo mameli . 23
Via goldoni . . . . . . . . . . 16
Via graziosa . . . . . . . . . . 7
Via gualtieri . . . . . . . . . 15
Via guardabassi . . . . . . 16
Via guerriera . . . . . . 16, 24
Via guerriero guerra . 20
Via guglielmo calderini
  16
Via guglielmo marconi
  24
Via guido pompili . . . . . 9
Via imbriani . . . . . . . . . . 17
Via ippolito nievo . . . . . . 9
Via italo svevo . . . . . . . . 9
Via l. bonazzi . . . . . 16, 24
Via laura . . . . . . . . . . . . . . 5

Via leon battista alberti
  9
Via leonardo da vinci 31,
  32
Via lino . . . . . . . . . . 10, 18
Via lorenzo maitani . . . . 9
Via lucida . . . . . . . . . . . . 7
Via ludovico ariosto . . 31
Via luigi canali . . . . . . . 22
Via luigi luzzatti . . . . . . 22
Via luigi menicucci . . . 16
Via luigi piastrelli . . . . . 29
Via luigi rizzo . . 20, 27, 28
Via luigi vanvitelli . . . . . 7
Via luisa spagnoli . 21, 28
Via lupatelli . . . . . . . . . . 7
Via lupattelli . . . . . . . . . 6
Via m. grecchi . . . . . . . 16
Via madonna alta 20, 21,
  26, 27
Via madonna del riccio 9
Via madonna di braccio
  25, 32
Via maestà delle volte
  16
Via magno magnini . 20,
  21
Via manara . . . . . . . . . . 23
Via manfredo fanti . . . 24
Via marcantonio bon-
  ciario . . . . . . . . . . . . 15
Via marchesi . . . . . . . . 18
Via marco polo . . . 12, 20
Via mariano piervittori . 5
Via mario angeloni 14, 22
Via mario santucci 33, 34
Via marsala . . . . . . . . . 29
Via martiri dei lager . . 21,
  28, 29
Via martiri di belfiore . 18
Via marzia . . . . . . . 16, 24
Via masi . . . . . . . . . . . . 24
Via mater dei . . . . . . . . 34
Via matteo gattapone . 9
Via matteo tassi . . . . . 4, 5
Via maturanzio . . . . . . 15
Via mentana . . . . . . 29–31
Via montemalbe . 12, 20,
  21
Via montemorcino . 5, 13,
  14
Via monteripido . . . . . . . 6
Via niccolò machiavelli
  31, 32
Via oberdan . . . . . . . . . 16
Via oddi sforza . . . . . . 22
Via orazio antinori . . 6, 15

Via orizzonte . . . . . . . . 17
Via orso . . . . . . . . . . . . 16
Via oscar scalvanti . . . 22
Via p. gobetti . . . . . . . . 27
Via p. ugolino nicolini . 6
Via palermo . . . . . . . . . 31
Via pazienza . . . . . . . . . 17
Via pellicciari . . . . . . . . 23
Via pericolosa . . . . . 7, 16
Via persico . . . . . . . . . . 25
Via piacevole . . . . . . . . . 7
Via piantarose . . . . 24, 25
Via pico della mirandola
  31, 32
Via pietro tuzi . . . . . 27, 28
Via pievaiola . . . . . 21, 22
Via pinturicchio . . . 16, 17
Via piscille . . . . . . . . . . 33
Via piscinello . . . . . . . . 15
Via podiani . . . . . . . . . . 24
Via pulcra . . . . . . . . . . . 17
Via pulignani . . . . . . . . . 7
Via quarto dei mille . . 29
Via quieta . . . . . . . . . . . 23
Via raffaele omicini . . 13,
  21, 22
Via raffaele silvestrini 28
Via raffaello . . . . . . . . . 17
Via raniero fasani . . . . 14
Via raniero gigliarelli . 13,
  14, 22
Via renata . . . . . . . . . . . 27
Via ritorta . . . . . . . . . . . 16
Via rodolfo betti . . . . . . 27
Via roma . . . . . . 24, 32, 33
Via romana . . . . . . . 33, 34
Via romeo gallenga . 20,
  21
Via ruggero d'andreotto
  14
Via ruggero torelli . . . . . 5
Via sabatina . . . . . . . . . 18
Via san bonaventura . 32
Via san costanzo . 32, 33
Via san domenico . . . . 25
Via san francesco . . . . 15
Via san galigano 4–6, 14,
  15
Via san giacomo . . 16, 24
Via san giovanni bosco
  17
Via san girolamo . 25, 39
Via san giuseppe . . . 8, 9
Via san manno . . . . . . 18
Via san prospero . 15, 22,
  23
Via san quirico . . . . . . 12

Via san savino . . . . . . . 24
Via san sebastiano . . . 16
Via san tommaso
    d'aquino . . . . . . . . 31
Via sant'agata . . . . . . . 16
Via sant'andrea . . . . . . 16
Via sant'anna . . . . . . . . 25
Via sant'anselmo
    d'aosta . . . . . . . . . 32
Via sant'ercolano . . . . . 16
Via santa elisabetta 7, 16
Via santa lucia . . 5, 13, 16
Via santa margherita . 17
Via santa scolastica . 26,
    27
Via santini . . . . . . . . . . . 5
Via scoscesa . . . . . . . . 16
Via scura . . . . . . . . . . . 16
Via sdrucciola . . . . . . . 17
Via seneca . . . . . . . 24, 31
Via serafino calindri . . . 5
Via serafino siepi . . 14, 15
Via sergio corazzini . . . 31
Via settevalli . . 22, 28, 29
Via severina . . . . . . . 21, 22
Via sicilia . . . . . . . . . . . 22
Via sidney costantino
    sonnino . . . . . . . . . 3

Via silvio pellico . . . . . . 32
Via simpatica . . . . . 21, 28
Via snella . . . . . . . . . . . . 17
Via solitaria . . . . . . . 16, 17
Via sottoripa . . . . . . . . 24
Via speciosa . . . . . . . . . 17
Via sperandio . . . . . . . 6, 7
Via stefania . . . . . . . 21, 22
Via tancredi ripa di
    meana . . . . . . . 17, 25
Via tazio nuvolari . . 10, 11
Via teano . . . . . . . . . . . 29
Via tedesca . . . . . . . . . . 7
Via terenzio mamiani 31,
    32
Via torcoletti . . . . . . . . 24
Via torelli . . . . . . . . . . 5, 14
Via tornitori . . . . . . . . . . 7
Via torricella . . . . . . . . . 17
Via tosca . . . . . . . . . . . 21
Via trasimeno ovest
    18–20
Via tuderte . . . . . . . 33, 34
Via ulisse rocchi . . . . . . 16
Via vanese . . . . . . . . . . 7
Via vermiglioli . . . . . . . . 16
Via vibi . . . . . . . . . . . . . 24
Via villa glori . . . . . . 14, 22

Via vincioli . . . . . . . . . . 16
Via vittorio alfieri . . . . . 32
Via volte della pace . 16,
    17
Via volumnia . . . . . 38, 39
Via xiv settembre . 16, 17,
    24, 25
Via xx settembre . . . . . 14,
    22–24
Via zefferino faina . . . 6, 7
Via zenobia . . . . . . . . . . 39
Viale centova . . . . . 19, 26
Viale dell'ingegneria . 10,
    11
Viale giovanni perari . 11,
    19, 20
Viale giuseppe meazza
    11
Viale indipendenza . . 16,
    24
Viale pietro conti . 10, 11,
    19
Viale pompeo pellini . 15,
    16
Viale roma . . . . 24, 25, 32
Viale sant'antonio 7, 8, 17
Volte della pace . . 16, 17

# Points of Interest

## A

Abbey San Pietro (Borgo XX Giugno 74) 🚶 . . . . . . . . . . . . 32
Arco Etrusco 🚶 . . . . . . 16

## B

Botanical Garden 🚶 . . 32
Braccio Lodge (Piazza IV Novembre 30) 🚶 16

## C

Capitini Train Station 🚆 18
Casa Monteripido (Students Dormitory) 🚶 6
Central Bus Station 🚌 24
Chapel San Severo (Piazza Raffello) 🏛 17
Church Filipo Neri 🚶 . 16
Church Saint Barnaba 🚶 21
Church Saint Francesco Al Prato 🚶 . . . . . . . 15
Church Sant'Ercolano 🚶 16
City Library and Church San Matteo degli Armeni 🚶 . . . . . . . . 6
Collegio del Cambio (Corso Vannucci 25) 🏛 . . . . . . . . . . . 16
Comune Perugia (Town Hall-Piazza Morlacchi) 🚶 . . . . . . . . . . . 16

Convent Oasi di Sant'Antonio 🚆 22

## G

Giuditta Brozzetti Museum - Weaving Workshop (Via Tiberio Berardi 5) 🏛 . . . . . . . . . . . . . . . . 6

## H

Hall of Notaries (Piazza IV Novembre 1) 🏛 16
House-Museum Palazzo Sorbello 🏛 . . . . . . . . . . . . . . . 16

## I

Ipogeo dei Volumni 🏛 38, 39

## J

Junior Tennis Club 🏃 . 23

## M

Madonna Alta 🖼 . . 20, 21
Monastery of Saint Caterina (Via Garibaldi 179) 🚶 7
Municipal Pool Pellini 🏃 15
Museum Calcio (F.C. Perugia) 🏛 . . . . . . 19

Museum Mura Urbiche (Corso Garibaldi) 🏛 6
Music Conservatory F. Morlacchi 🚶 . . . . . 15

## O

Oratory of Saint Bernardino 🚶 . . . . 15

## P

Palasport Evangelisti 🏃 11
Palazzine Antiquarium Necropolis 🏛 . . . 39
Palazzine Necropolis 🚶 38, 39
Palazzo dei Priori (Corso Vannuci 19) 🚶 . . . 16
Palazzo Della Penna Civic Museum (Via Prospero Podiani 11) 🏛 . . . . . . . . . . . . 24
Palazzo Donini (Piazza Italia) 🚶 . . . . . . . . . . 16
Parish San Raffaele Arcangelo 🚶 . . . . . . 27
Park Percorso Verde 🚶 10
Perugia Train Station 🚆 22
Perugia University - Veterinary Faculty and Hospital 🏛 . 33
Perugia University 🏛 . 6, 7, 16
Perugia University for Foreigners Campus 🏛 . . . . . . . . . . . 17

48

Made in the USA
Middletown, DE
09 November 2021